D1717037

BATTLE OF
HASTINGS

BY JOHN HAMILTON

VISIT US AT
WWW.ABDOPUBLISHING.COM

Published by ABDO Publishing Company, PO Box 398166, Minneapolis, MN 55439. Copyright ©2014 by Abdo Consulting Group, Inc. International copyrights reserved in all countries. No part of this book may be reproduced in any form without written permission from the publisher. ABDO & Daughters™ is a trademark and logo of ABDO Publishing Company.

Printed in the United States of America, North Mankato, Minnesota.
122013
012014

 PRINTED ON RECYCLED PAPER

Editor: Sue Hamilton
Graphic Design: Sue Hamilton
Cover Design: Neil Klinepier
Cover Photo: Stephen Moss-UK
Interior Images: Alamy-pgs 9, 11, 12, 13, 14, 15, 21, 22 & 26; Bayeux Tapestry-pgs 1, 8 (bottom) & 16; Corbis-pg 17; Getty Images-pgs 6, 18 & 19; Glow Images-pgs 4-5, 10, 24, 27 & 29; Granger Collection-pg 23; John Hamilton-pgs 7 & 20; Thinkstock-All backgrounds & pg 25; University of Cambridge/Cambridge Digital Library-pg 8 (top); Wikimedia-pg 28.

ABDO Booklinks
To learn more about Great Battles, visit ABDO Publishing Company online. Web sites about Great Battles are featured on our Booklinks pages. These links are routinely monitored and updated to provide the most current information available. Web site: www.abdopublishing.com

Library of Congress Control Number: 2013946973

Cataloging-in-Publication Data

Hamilton, John, 1959-
  Battle of Hastings / John Hamilton.
    p. cm. -- (Great battles)
  Includes index.
  ISBN 978-1-62403-204-2
  1. Hastings, Battle of, England, 1066--Juvenile literature. I. Title.
  942.02--dc23

2013946973

CONTENTS

THE BATTLE FOR A
KINGDOM

On a crisp autumn morning in the year 1066, two huge armies faced off against each other on a hill in southern England. At the crest of the hill stood Harold Godwinson, the king of England, together with thousands of his fierce Anglo-Saxon warriors. Facing the Englishmen was a hoard of foreign invaders—Normans from across the English Channel. They were led by William I, the Duke of Normandy, whose ruthlessness in battle was matched only by his ambition.

As the two sides waited, foot soldiers beat their shields with the pommels of their swords. Their war cries echoed up and down the English countryside. Norman cavalry stood ready, the horses snorting steam into the morning air.

Archers nocked their arrows, awaiting the order to attack.

The Battle of Hastings was about to begin. The winner's prize: the throne of England.

The battle would be one of the largest and bloodiest in medieval history. Its outcome would forever change the history of Great Britain.

Harold Godwinson's Anglo-Saxon warriors battle William I's Norman invaders.

KEY EVENTS BEFORE THE
BATTLE

In 1066, the year the Battle of Hastings was fought, England was ruled by people called Anglo-Saxons. Much earlier, from about 40 to 410 A.D., the land was part of the Roman Empire, and was named Britannia, or Britain. After the Romans left in the 5th century, large parts of the south of Britain were invaded by warriors from present-day northern Germany and Denmark. They were the Saxons and Angles. It is from the Angles

The coronation of Edward the Confessor in 1042.

that we get the modern name for the south of Britain: England.

Over a period of hundreds of years, the Anglo-Saxon people formed their own small kingdoms, which were spread all over England. Eventually, they combined their powers until there was a single nation, the Kingdom of England. The country was ruled by King Edward the Confessor from 1042 until 1066.

King Edward was called "the Confessor" because he was deeply religious. He prayed a lot, and built many churches, including the first version of Westminster Abbey. Edward was born in England, but he had a much different background than the Anglo-Saxon people he ruled. The king spent most of his childhood and early adult years in Normandy, the land where his mother came from. Normandy was a part of France. About 150 years earlier, the French king gave Normandy to a group of invading Vikings to rule, in exchange for peace. (The word "Normandy" came from a common name for a Viking—Northman, a man from the north.) Normandy was a duchy, or territory, of France. It was ruled by a duke who was loyal to the French king. In time, the Normans adapted to their new homeland and had families with the local citizens. They kept their warrior traditions, and many became powerful knights on horseback.

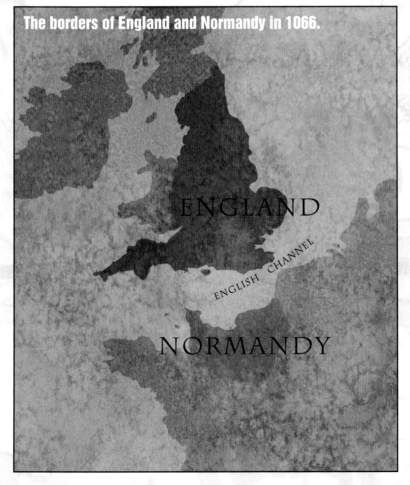

The borders of England and Normandy in 1066.

ENGLAND

ENGLISH CHANNEL

NORMANDY

In 1041, Edward returned to England. The following year, he began his reign as King Edward the Confessor. Because of his ties to his mother's homeland, some of the

King Edward begins his reign in 1042.

king's closest advisors were from Normandy, and many of the castles and churches he built used Norman architecture. However, he was an English king first and foremost, who used his energy and ruthlessness to benefit his Anglo-Saxon subjects.

On January 5, 1066, after a long and mostly peaceful rule, Edward the Confessor was on his deathbed. A huge problem gripped the land. Edward had no heirs to pass his crown to. Who would be the next king?

Across the English Channel in France, there was one man who thought he knew the answer to that question: William, the powerful Duke of Normandy. William and Edward the Confessor were distant cousins, and had known each other when the English king lived in Normandy. William claimed that Edward had promised him the throne of England upon his death.

The death of Edward the Confessor (lower right corner) on January 5, 1066.

In England, the Anglo-Saxon nobility was not about to let a foreign-born duke take over their country. When Edward the Confessor died, they quickly named Harold Godwinson, a powerful politician and nobleman, as their next king. Harold took the throne on January 6, 1066.

When news of Harold's coronation reached William in Normandy, the duke was outraged. He claimed that Harold had years earlier made a sacred oath that only he, William, could claim the throne of England, fulfilling the promise of Edward the Confessor. Harold had broken that oath, and as far as Duke William was concerned, had made a declaration of war. The duke prepared his army for what would become the most famous battle ever fought on English soil.

When William discovered that Harold Godwinson had been named king of England in 1066, he was outraged. William believed that he was to be the next king. He prepared his army for battle.

THE BATTLE'S
LEADERS

William, the Duke of Normandy (1028-1087), was born around 1028 in Falaise, Normandy. He was a descendent of Viking invaders who came to northern France in the early 900s. He became duke in 1035 after the death of his father, Duke Robert I. Because he was only about seven years old at the time, his great uncle ran the affairs of Normandy until William was old enough to handle the responsibilities.

Many high-ranking people in Normandy wanted power for themselves, and were willing to resort to violence to achieve their goals. At least three of William's guardians were murdered, one in William's bedroom while the young duke slept. Each time, William escaped harm.

William, the Duke of Normandy

In 1047, William smashed a rebellion among his own Norman nobles. Over the next decade, his thirst for power grew. He began to expand his lands and political influence.

On the battlefield, William was a skilled fighter and horseman. He was tall and burly, and was able to draw bows that were too tight for most men. He loved to hunt. He could be cruel to his enemies, but loyal to his friends. He was also deeply religious, and relied on the clergy for advice and political influence.

King Harold Godwinson (1022-1066) ruled England after the death of Edward the Confessor in 1066. Born about 1022, Harold came from a rich family of English landowners. He had close political ties to King Edward. (He was also the king's brother-in-law.)

As the Earl of Wessex (in the southern part of England), Harold was second only to King Edward in wealth and power. He was also skilled in warfare. Not only did he lead men into battle, Harold often fought on the front lines, swinging his axe in the defense of his kingdom.

Harold made alliances with all the major nobles in the kingdom. When Edward died, Harold was in the strongest political position to become the next king of England, even though he had no English royal blood. The day after Edward's death, on January 6, 1066, he was crowned King Harold II, ruler of England. He would be the last of the Saxon kings.

King Harold Godwinson

TACTICS AND WEAPONS

The weapons used by the armies of England's King Harold and Normandy's Duke William were similar in many ways. Most soldiers of the Middle Ages relied on bladed weapons, such as swords and axes. Clubs were also used. Fighting was brutal. Enemy soldiers were either slashed or beaten to death. Opposing armies generally lined up against each other and fought hand-to-hand until one side gave way and crumbled. When small pockets of enemy troops could be isolated from the main

A reenactor wears a helmet and chain mail, and holds a sword.

group, they were surrounded and killed. When an army's line disintegrated completely, the survivors had no choice but to flee for their lives.

Most troops wore some type of body armor. A tunic, or long coat, of hard leather was often all that stood between a soldier and the enemy's blade. The richest soldiers wore garments made of small iron rings interlocked together. Today we call this armor "chain mail," but medieval people simply called it mail. It protected soldiers from most cutting blows, such as from swords.

Mail armor was made into shirts, hoods, leggings, and gloves. A full suit could weigh as much as 65 pounds (29 kg). Warriors had to be strong and agile to wear heavy mail in battle.

Shields protected soldiers not only from bladed weapons, but also from arrows. Most English shields were round. Norman knights preferred shields that were kite-shaped. The extra length protected the legs.

Medieval shields were made of layers of thick wooden boards glued together, like plywood. The wood was covered with a hard material, such as leather or plaster. The outside of many shields were colorfully decorated, sometimes with a knight's coat of arms.

English armies used their round shields in a way that gave them a big advantage when they were being attacked. The soldiers stood shoulder-to-shoulder and interlocked their shields together, creating a long, solid wall of defense against the enemy. These "shield walls" were very effective and difficult to break. As the enemy pressed against a shield wall, they were attacked with spears or axes by soldiers standing safely behind the shields.

Reenactors create an English "shield wall" by interlocking their round shields.

Some English soldiers were armed with two-handed axes, while others used swords and spears.

The favorite cutting weapon of the English army was the two-handed axe. They were used by professional soldiers called housecarls, a Scandinavian word that means a servant, or bodyguard, of a lord. King Harold had several thousand of these elite housecarls at his service. Their axes were several feet long, with metal heads large enough to chop off limbs, or even a horse's head, with a single blow. The disadvantage of the axe was that it required two hands to wield. When raised over the head to strike, it left a soldier's front exposed to sword or spear attacks.

Norman soldiers preferred swords. They could be very expensive, often passed down as heirlooms from generation to generation. Although they came in many shapes and sizes, most swords weighed less than three pounds (1.4 kg). They were used to slash at the enemy, or crush his bones, even through mail armor. The sharp point of the blade was used for stabbing. The knob-like end of the sword's grip, the pommel, could be used like a hammer.

Duke William had many archers at the Battle of Hastings. King Harold had a few men armed with bows and arrows, but not nearly as many as the Normans. Massed arrow attacks were fearsome. Arrows could be shot from across a battlefield, and often pierced mail armor. Soldiers tried to deflect arrow attacks with their shields, but many were killed or wounded by these flying daggers.

Duke William had another weapon at his disposal: knights who fought on horseback. The duke's cavalry were the most feared and well-trained knights in all of Europe. They could quickly ride around the battlefield and attack as needed with spears and swords. The horses were also used as weapons. The animals were trained to trample enemy troops, and even to bite. A massed charge of Norman knights caused fear among even the most battle-hardened foot soldier. England's army had horses also, but they were only used to transport men and supplies. When English soldiers reached the battlefield, they fought on foot.

Archers could shoot across the battlefield.

THE NORMANS PREPARE TO INVADE

In April 1066, Halley's Comet appeared in the night sky. Many superstitious Europeans viewed this strange, once-in-a-lifetime astronomical event as a sign of unrest. They thought the comet's appearance was somehow connected to the leadership crisis in England.

Halley's Comet (upper right) in the Bayeux Tapestry.

Outraged that the English throne had not been given to him as promised, Normandy's Duke William began assembling his army and made plans to invade England. Unfortunately, the duke didn't have enough men. He sought help from Pope Alexander II. Popes in the Middle Ages were much more powerful than they are today. Pope Alexander sided with Duke William, and let him carry into battle a papal banner, a kind of flag that demonstrated the support of the Church. William's quest to take over the English throne became an official crusade. Knights from all over Europe, even as far away as Italy, flocked to William's army. They were drawn to battle by the promise of land, money, and a place in the afterlife.

By August, William had assembled about 7,000 soldiers. He built hundreds of ships to carry his army, including weapons, supplies, and horses, across the English Channel. The invasion, however, was delayed because of something even the powerful Duke of Normandy couldn't control: the weather. Unfavorable winds meant that the Norman ships were stuck in port. All William and his army could do was wait.

Vikings burn and raid a Saxon village.

Meanwhile, in England, King Harold had a pretty good idea that Duke William's invasion force was coming. To protect England's southern coast, King Harold called out the fyrd. The fyrd were a kind of local militia, not professional soldiers. The king could call them to service, armed with their own weapons and supplies, for a two-month term of enlistment. Harold stationed the fyrd along the coast to repel whatever Norman invasion might appear.

Weeks passed with no sign of Duke William and his invading Norman army. King Harold reluctantly allowed most of the fyrd to disband so they could return home and attend to their harvests.

King Harold fretted. What had become of the Norman invasion? Soon, however, the king learned of another threat to his kingdom. An invading army had landed on England's northeastern coast and was burning and pillaging villages. This was not the long-feared Norman invasion, but something just as alarming—Vikings!

THE BATTLE OF STAMFORD BRIDGE

In September 1066, England's King Harold was suddenly faced with two invasions at once. In the south, he feared the army of Normandy's Duke William

The Norman fleet sails for England in September 1066.

would soon arrive. But to the north, he received word that thousands of Vikings had already landed on England's eastern coast. They were led by King Harald Hardrada of Norway. Worse still, the English king's own younger brother, Tostig Godwinson, had joined forces with the invaders. The traitor Tostig, who had been exiled by his brother, convinced the Viking king to attack and seize the English throne.

Caught off balance, King Harold gathered as many men as possible and hurried to the north. He traveled from London to the county of Yorkshire, almost 200 miles (322 km), in only four days. Harold's army caught the Vikings totally by surprise. At the Battle of Stamford Bridge, the English army destroyed the invasion force. The fighting was brutal. Both Harald of Norway and Tostig were killed, ending the Viking threat.

During the Battle of Stamford Bridge, King Harold's English army destroyed the Viking invaders.

Meanwhile, in the south, favorable winds allowed Duke William to finally set sail for the south of England. His Norman army landed on September 28. The Normans were shocked to find only light resistance. They built fortifications near the coastal town of Hastings and then began raiding the surrounding countryside.

When news of Duke William's long-awaited invasion reached King Harold, he quickly packed up and returned south. Even though his army was exhausted after fighting the Vikings, he and his men made haste to meet the new threat.

After gathering fresh forces in London, the English army marched back to the south coast, arriving in just a few days.

King Harold set up his defenses along a ridge called Senlac Hill, a few miles north of Hastings (near the present-day town of Battle, England). It was a good defensive position. The area behind was heavily wooded. Steep slopes protected the English flanks (sides). The hill was astride a major road. Harold knew that Duke William and his army would travel through the area on their way to London. The English king was ready for battle.

THE BATTLE OF HASTINGS

As the sun rose on the morning of October 14, 1066, Duke William of Normandy stood at the bottom of Senlac Hill and gazed up at the massive English army blocking his path to London. The army of his enemy, King Harold, had an excellent defensive position. Harold's approximately 7,000 men had formed a shield wall. Warriors in front stood shoulder-to-shoulder and overlapped their shields to create a solid wall of defense. The line was several men deep, with soldiers in back wielding spears, axes, and clubs against anyone who dared attack the shield wall.

Duke William also had about 7,000 men in his army. They were comprised of soldiers from all over Europe, although the bulk of them were from Normandy. William divided his army into three groups. On the left flank (side) was a group of about 2,000 Bretons (from the French region of Brittany). On the right flank were about 1,500 Flemish soldiers (from

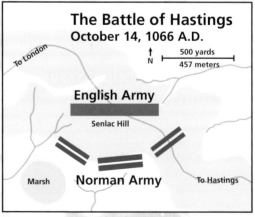

The Battle of Hastings
October 14, 1066 A.D.

500 yards
457 meters

To London

English Army

Senlac Hill

Norman Army

Marsh

To Hastings

Reenactors clash in a historical recreation of the Battle of Hastings in England.

Flanders, in present-day northern Belgium). The largest group was in the center. It contained several thousand Norman warriors led personally by Duke William.

At 9:00 a.m., a trumpet sounded, signaling the beginning of the battle. About 1,500 Norman archers sent a shower of arrows uphill toward the English army. The attack failed, with most of the arrows plunking into shields or sailing harmlessly overhead.

Next, William sent his infantry and cavalry to attack. After trudging up the hill toward the terrifying sight of the enemy army, the Norman footmen and knights crashed against the English shield wall. The fighting was ferocious. English axes, swords, and spears cut down the Norman attackers, and the shield wall held tight.

21

After an hour of bloody hand-to-hand fighting, a large group of Breton soldiers on Duke William's left flank began to waver. As more and more dead began to pile up, fear gripped the men. They broke ranks and ran back down the slope. Some of the English soldiers sensed victory. They left the safety of the shield wall and pursued the Normans down the hill.

To make matters worse, Duke William fell off his horse. A rumor swept through the Norman troops that their leader was dead. The men began to panic. William acted quickly to regain control of his army. He remounted his horse and raised his helmet. He galloped through his troops and shouted, "Look at me! I am alive, and by the grace of God we'll be the victor!"

Duke William raises his helmet to show his Norman troops that he is alive.

William and his Norman horsemen isolate and slaughter English foot soldiers.

William then led a counterattack with his cavalry against the English soldiers who were pursuing the retreating Bretons. The swift cavalry surrounded the isolated enemy troops and killed them.

Seeing their leader alive rallied the Norman troops. They attacked again in waves, but each time the English shield wall held firm. By now it was midafternoon, and the ground of Senlac Hill was slippery with blood. Hundreds of dead soldiers lie strewn about the battlefield. Duke William called for a general retreat so that his men could regroup and rest.

At the crest of the hill, English King Harold looked down on his enemy with satisfaction. He had suffered many losses, but his men had not broken under the Norman onslaught. If his army could hold out until the evening, his chances for total victory would improve. Fresh reinforcements were on their way and would reach the battlefield by morning. He was determined to outlast the Norman threat and send the invaders back across the sea, or kill them all in the process.

Duke William leads his cavalry in an attack against the English line.

By late afternoon, Duke William had lost about one-quarter of his army, almost 2,000 men. William started to use trickery to weaken the enemy. He sent groups of men to attack the English line and then pretend to run away. The excited English troops, as before, broke ranks and ran down the hill in pursuit. William's cavalry promptly surrounded the isolated enemy and slaughtered them. This ploy worked several times, but did not achieve victory. Time after time, King Harold was able to plug the holes in his defenses, and the English shield wall held.

As the sun began to set, William knew that time was running out. He decided to make one final, combined attack on the English line. He preceded the assault with a barrage from his archers, but this time ordered them to aim high, so that the arrows fell down almost vertically upon the English troops's heads. Then, the Norman infantry and cavalry made one last all-out attack. The fighting was brutal and desperate. There were breaks in

King Harold is struck by an arrow shot from an unknown Norman archer.

the English shield wall, but many Normans were killed in the attack also. Both sides sensed that victory was at hand. For William, defeat would mean almost certain death. And then, calamity struck the English side.

A stray arrow shot from an unknown Norman archer struck King Harold in the eye. The mortally wounded king was then hacked to death by sword-wielding Normans. In medieval battles, the death of a leader almost always meant defeat. The English army wavered and then finally collapsed. Some fled into the nearby forests. Many were hunted down by William's troops and killed. The Norman duke had achieved a decisive victory, and the English king had lost not only his crown, but also his life. After one of the longest, bloodiest fights in medieval history, the Battle of Hastings was finally over.

THE BATTLE'S AFTERMATH

Nobody knows where English King Harold is buried. His body was so badly mangled that he was not officially identified. It's possible he was recognized by relatives and buried near the sea. More likely, he was put to rest in a nameless grave along with other soldiers killed in the Battle of Hastings. The combined losses of both sides were approximately 4,000 to 6,000 men killed that day. Whatever really happened to Harold may never be

William's victory at the Battle of Hastings.

known. What is certain is that the reign of Anglo-Saxon kings in England had come to an end.

Although the Battle of Hastings was a great victory for Duke William, his struggle to seize control of England continued for another two months. The surviving English leaders were determined to fight the Norman invasion. William responded by roaming throughout southeastern England, burning towns and crushing resistance wherever he found it.

Riots erupted between Norman soldiers and London townspeople as William was crowned the new king of England inside Westminster Abbey on December 25, 1066.

Finally, the English accepted their fate. On Christmas Day, 1066, William was crowned the new king of England in Westminster Abbey, London. From that day forward, he would forever be known as William the Conqueror.

The Norman conquest had far-reaching effects on England. It linked England with the rest of Europe. French became the official language of government, and English people were forbidden to hold many jobs. Normans controlled the nobles and the Church. The language of the Anglo-Saxons, Old English (which resembled German or Scandinavian), began to be replaced by the modern English language we understand today. A great many English words spoken today have French origin, such as *art*, *police*, and *garden*. Despite these many changes, the Normans did keep many superior English institutions, including systems of government and banking.

When William the Conqueror died in 1087, the crown of England was passed down to his son, also named William. For many generations, the throne was held by foreign-born kings. Over hundreds of years, the two cultures blended. Normans intermarried with the local population. Eventually, the kings, like their subjects, became a people that we recognize today as "English."

THE BAYEUX TAPESTRY

One of the reasons we know so much today about the Battle of Hastings is because of a piece of artwork called the Bayeux Tapestry. It is a colorful embroidered cloth that is almost 230 feet (70 m) long, and about 1.6 feet (.5 m) wide. Like a medieval graphic novel, it depicts the Battle of Hastings, and the events leading up to the battle, in 50 scenes narrated in Latin.

It was believed that William the Conqueror's wife, Queen Matilda, and her ladies-in-waiting embroidered the Bayeux Tapestry. However, it is now thought that the artwork was probably commissioned by William's half-brother, Bishop Odo.

The Bayeux Tapestry depicts the Battle of Hastings, as well as the events leading up to the battle. Now more than 950 years old, it is on display in Bayeux, France.

Stitched with eight different shades of woolen yarn onto pieces of linen, the Bayeux Tapestry is not a true tapestry (in which the designs are actually woven into the fabric). Its creation was probably ordered by Bishop Odo, William the Conqueror's half brother, in the 1070s. Constructed and stitched by skilled artisans in England, it was then moved to the city of Bayeux, Normandy, France, and displayed in Bayeux Cathedral. Remarkably, it has survived almost 950 years of history mostly intact.

The Bayeux Tapestry doesn't necessarily tell the whole story of the battle. It only tells the side of the winners, the Norman invaders. Historians try to double check the artwork's story with other documents written at the time, like the *Anglo-Saxon Chronicle*, which was written by English monks. However, in many cases the Bayeux Tapestry is the only source of what we know about the Battle of Hastings.

GLOSSARY

ANGLO-SAXON

The Germanic/Scandinavian people who dominated England from the time of their arrival in the 5th century until the Norman Conquest of 1066.

CAVALRY

Historically, soldiers who rode and fought on horseback were called cavalry. Modern cavalry includes soldiers who fight in armored vehicles such as tanks or attack helicopters.

COAT OF ARMS

A unique design that distinguishes a person, family, or country. In medieval times, knights painted a coat of arms onto their shields or outer garments in order to be identified in battle.

ENGLISH CHANNEL

The sea channel between northern France and southern England. At its narrowest section, it is only 22 miles (35 m) wide.

HOUSECARL

A bodyguard of an English lord or noble. Also, a professional soldier.

MEDIEVAL

Something from the Middle Ages.

MIDDLE AGES

In European history, a period defined by historians as roughly between 476 A.D. and 1450 A.D.

MILITIA

Citizens who are part-time soldiers rather than professional army fighters. King Harold's English fyrd were a kind of local militia.

NOBLE

Someone born into a class of people who have high social or political status. Sometimes ordinary people can be made nobles by doing something extraordinary, like fighting well on the battlefield. Usually, however, only people who are the sons or daughters of nobles get to be nobles themselves.

ROMAN EMPIRE

The ancient civilization centered in Rome, in present-day Italy. The western Roman Empire lasted from 27 B.C. until 476 A.D. Led by a series of emperors who held great power, the Roman Empire at its height stretched over most of Europe, plus large sections of northern Africa and western Asia.

TAPESTRY

A piece of thick fabric with pictures or designs that are woven into the cloth. They are used as wall hangings or to cover furniture. They helped keep out cold drafts that blew through castle walls. Medieval tapestries often displayed scenes of historical significance.

WESTMINSTER ABBEY

A large church in the City of Westminster, London, England. Although the abbey was the site of other churches since at least the 7th century, the present church was built starting in 1245 during the reign of King Henry III. The coronations of English kings and queens, as well as many royal weddings, are held at Westminster Abbey. Many nobles and other important persons are buried there as well.

INDEX